BACKYARD WILDLIFE

# Hawks

by Kari Schuetz

BELLWETHER MEDIA · MINNEAPOLIS, MN

Note to Librarians, Teachers, and Parents:

**Blastoff! Readers** are carefully developed by literacy experts and combine standards-based content with developmentally appropriate text.

**Level 1** provides the most support through repetition of high-frequency words, light text, predictable sentence patterns, and strong visual support.

**Level 2** offers early readers a bit more challenge through varied simple sentences, increased text load, and less repetition of high-frequency words.

**Level 3** advances early-fluent readers toward fluency through increased text and concept load, less reliance on visuals, longer sentences, and more literary language.

**Level 4** builds reading stamina by providing more text per page, increased use of punctuation, greater variation in sentence patterns, and increasingly challenging vocabulary.

**Level 5** encourages children to move from "learning to read" to "reading to learn" by providing even more text, varied writing styles, and less familiar topics.

Whichever book is right for your reader, Blastoff! Readers are the perfect books to build confidence and encourage a love of reading that will last a lifetime!

This edition first published in 2014 by Bellwether Media, Inc.

No part of this publication may be reproduced in whole or in part without written permission of the publisher. For information regarding permission, write to Bellwether Media, Inc., Attention: Permissions Department, 5357 Penn Avenue South, Minneapolis, MN 55419.

Library of Congress Cataloging-in-Publication Data

Schuetz, Kari.
  Hawks / by Kari Schuetz.
    pages cm. – (Blastoff! Readers: Backyard Wildlife)
  Summary: "Developed by literacy experts for students in kindergarten through grade three, this book introduces hawks to young readers through leveled text and related photos"– Provided by publisher.
  Audience: Ages 5-8.
  Audience: K to grade 3.
  Includes bibliographical references and index.
  ISBN 978-1-62617-058-2 (hardcover : alk. paper)
  1. Hawks–Juvenile literature.  I. Title.
  QL696.F32S32 2014
  598.9'44–dc23
                                        2013037612

Printed in the United States of America, North Mankato, MN.

# Contents

Hawks are **raptors**. They are large birds that hunt.

Hawks search for **prey** in grasslands, forests, and **deserts**. They hunt from the sky and **perches**.

Hawks can spot prey from far away. They see eight times better than people!

They swoop down
to grab mice, rabbits,
and other small
animals. They use
their strong **talons**.

talons

Then hawks use their **hooked** beaks to tear apart their meals.

Most hawks make nests high up in trees. They build them out of sticks.

Female hawks lay between one and five eggs in a nest. They stay to **incubate** the eggs.

Male hawks protect the eggs. They also bring food to the females.

19

Chicks **hatch** after about 30 days. They leave the nest when they can fly. Takeoff time!

# Glossary

**deserts**—dry lands with little rain

**hatch**—to break out of an egg

**hooked**—sharp and curved

**incubate**—to keep warm; hawks sit on their eggs to incubate them until chicks hatch.

**perches**—tree branches and other high places; birds sit on perches to watch for prey or rest.

**prey**—animals that are hunted by other animals for food

**raptors**—birds that hunt other animals for food

**talons**—sharp claws on the feet of raptors

# To Learn More

## AT THE LIBRARY

McCarthy, Meghan. *City Hawk: The Story of Pale Male*. New York, N.Y.: Simon and Schuster Books for Young Readers, 2007.

Schuetz, Kari. *Birds*. Minneapolis, Minn.: Bellwether Media, 2013.

Sill, Cathryn. *About Raptors: A Guide for Children*. Atlanta, Ga.: Peachtree Publishers, 2010.

## ON THE WEB

Learning more about hawks is as easy as 1, 2, 3.

1. Go to www.factsurfer.com.

2. Enter "hawks" into the search box.

3. Click the "Surf" button and you will see a list of related Web sites.

With factsurfer.com, finding more information is just a click away.

# Index

The images in this book are reproduced through the courtesy of: Voisin/ Phanie/ SuperStock, front cover; Thomas Barrat, p. 5; Paul Reeves Photography, p. 7; Spirit of America, p. 7 (bottom right); Chris Geszvain, p. 7 (bottom middle); Anton Foltin, p. 7 (bottom right); kungverylucky, p. 9; Jukka Palm, p. 11; CreativeNature, p. 11 (bottom left); Pim Leijen, p. 11 (bottom right); david tipling/ Image Broker/ SuperStock, p. 13; Franz Christoph Robiller/ Image Broker/ SuperStock/ Glow Images, pp. 15, 17; Mark Hamblin/ age fotostock, p. 19; Wayne Lynch/ All Canada Photos/ Superstock, p. 21.